QUICK & EASY
Entrees with Style

Edie Hand • Darlene Real • Debra Lustrea

Nomad Press
A division of Nomad Communications
10 9 8 7 6 5 4 3 2 1
Copyright © 2003 Nomad Communications
All rights reserved.

No part of this book may be reproduced in any form without permission in writing the publisher, except by a reviewer who may quote brief passages in a review. The trademark "Nomad Press" and the Nomad Press logo are trademarks of Nomad Communications, Inc. Printed in Canada.

ISBN 0-9722026-1-7

Questions regarding the ordering of this book for the trade should be addressed
Independent Publishers Group
814 N. Franklin St.
Chicago, IL 60610
or for individuals go to: www.nomadpress.net

Interior illustrations by Jeff McAllister
Design by Jeff McAllister
Edited by Susan Hale and Lauri Berkenkamp

Nomad Press, PO Box 875, Norwich, VT 05055

Table of Contents

Recipes

Salmon Patties 2
On-the-Run Tuna Melts 4
Edie's Mushroom and Chicken Delight 6
Microwave Ham Casserole 8
Seafood Gumbo 10
Spicy Chicken Chowder 12
Greek Burgers 14
Poached Salmon 16
Country-Style Chicken Kiev 18
Chicken a la King 20
Irresistible Pork Chops 22
Asparagus-Chicken Parmesan 24
Eggplant Parmesan 26
Chicken Breasts with Swiss Cheese 28
Chicken Tenders 30

Herb and Lemon Fried Chicken 32
Lemon Chicken 34
Dijon Fish 36
Asian Beef 38
Prime Rib Roast with Garlic 40
Sirloin Burgers 42
Southern Meatloaf 44
Moore's Marinade™ Mushrooms 46
Shrimp Pecan Vegetable Pilau 48
Beer-Battered Fried Shrimp and Vegetables 50
Greek Eggplant, Tomato, and Feta Pizza 52
Spaghetti with Marinara Sauce 54
Ginger Broiled Fish 58
Roast Pork with Sweet Potato Treat 60
Zucchini Sausage Bake 62
Cornmeal Pancakes 64
Seafood Bake 66

Quick and Easy Grits with Sausage Rolls 68
Healthy Way Omelet 70
Vegetable Bread 72
Spinach Lasagna 74
Zesty Grilled Chicken 76
Beef and Rice 78

Etiquette and Style
Place Settings 82
The Basics of Dining Etiquette 86

Know Your Ingredients
Conversion Tables 90
Recipe Modifications/Substitutions 92
Exchanges and Nutrition Tips 94

Dear Friends,

Over 15 million Americans are affected by Type 2 diabetes. So many of us live with diabetes, or know someone — friend, family member, or colleague — who has the disease. Both of my grandmothers, two nieces, and a nephew live with, or have lived with, the complications of some form of diabetes for many years. I am pleased to help raise awareness of the importance of eating healthier through the *Food, Family & Friends* cookbook series.

You'll find some of my favorite recipes in this cookbook. Some are generously provided by the Heart College at HealthSouth in Birmingham, Alabama. Debra and I have offered our treasured family recipes, with adaptations to make them more diabetic friendly. A few come from an earlier book of mine, *Recipes for Life*, also with diabetic adaptations in mind. Enjoy—and remember to exercise, eat right, and get lots of rest. We are all in this together.

—Edie Hand

Note: Consult with your physician or your local Diabetes Association Chapter for a healthy lifestyle plan.

Diabetes contact information:

American Diabetes Association: www.diabetes.org or 800-DIABETES

American Dietetic Association: Nutritional information hotline at 800-366-1655

Diabetes Trust Fund: Research information at www.diabetestrustfund.org or 800-577-1383

Juvenile Diabetes: www.childrenwithdiabetes.com

Recipes

Salmon Patties

- 1   16-ounce can salmon
- ¼   cup self-rising flour (or all-purpose flour and ¼ teaspoon baking powder)
- 2   eggs, beaten
- 1   medium onion, chopped
- 1½ cups crushed Saltines
- ¼   cup finely chopped green pepper
- 1   dash garlic powder
- 1   cup olive oil, for frying

Remove the skin and bone (if necessary) from the salmon, and place salmon in a mixing bowl. Mash the salmon to separate it slightly. Add the flour, eggs, onion, Saltines, green pepper, and garlic powder. Stir until well blended.

Form the mixture into balls in the palm of your hand, using about 2½ ounces to form 8 balls. In a skillet, heat 1½ inches of oil on medium-high heat. Drop the balls into the oil and fry until brown. Drain in a colander, then on paper towels. Makes 8 patties.

Kids Tip
Children will love to help create this old favorite. Let your children crush the crackers, beat the eggs, and form the balls. However, dropping the croquettes into the hot oil should be an adults-only activity.

Nutritional Information

Information per serving (8 servings)

Calories	142	Percentage of Calories from Carbohydrates: 25%
Carbohydrates	9 gm	Percentage of Calories from Protein: 37%
Protein	13 gm	Percentage of Calories from Fat: 38%
Fat	6 gm	
Cholesterol	77 mg	**Diabetic Food Exchange**
Sodium	335 mg	Carbohydrate: 0.5
Fiber	0 gm	Protein: 2
Calcium	139 mg	Fat: 1
Iron	1 mg	
Vitamin A	170 IU	
Vitamin C	1 mg	

Real Style

The secret to great taste and the visual appeal of this recipe is to drain the oil from the croquettes on paper towels. Roll over each croquette a couple of times before placing on a platter or plate. This will make them look crispy rather than soggy.

Place croquettes, pyramid style, on a painted pottery platter. Tuck parsley in spaces and alternate with lemon wedges and parsley around the bottom of the stacked croquettes. Use an old kitchen mixing bowl, ceramic or wooden, for an impromptu vase for assorted wildflowers.

On-the-Run Tuna Melts

1. 6-ounce can water-packed solid white tuna, drained and flaked
- ¾ cup chopped celery
- 2 tablespoons finely chopped onion
- ½ teaspoon grated lemon peel, if desired
- ⅓ cup fat-free mayonnaise or salad dressing
- 4 whole-wheat English muffins, split, lightly toasted
- 8 slices of tomato
- 4 ounces (1 cup) shredded, reduced-fat Cheddar or Monterey Jack cheese

Heat the oven to 350°F.

In a medium bowl, combine tuna, celery, onion, lemon peel, and mayonnaise. Mix well. Spread about 3 tablespoons tuna mixture on each English muffin half. Top each with a tomato slice, and sprinkle with cheese.

Place on an ungreased cookie sheet. Bake for 8–10 minutes or until cheese is melted and sandwiches are thoroughly heated. Serves 8.

Nutritional Information

Information per serving (8 servings)

Calories	125	
Carbohydrates	15 gm	
Protein	11 gm	
Fat	2 gm	
Cholesterol	10 mg	
Sodium	342 mg	
Fiber	1 gm	
Calcium	119 mg	
Iron	1 mg	
Vitamin A	68 IU	
Vitamin C	3 mg	

Percentage of Calories from Carbohydrates: 49%
Percentage of Calories from Protein: 36%
Percentage of Calories from Fat: 15%

Diabetic Food Exchange
Carbohydrates: 1
Protein: 2
Fat: 0

Real Style

When it comes to jet-speed entrees, this is at the top of the list, way ahead of fast foods. You can dress this Melt up for dinner by placing the muffin half on a dinner plate, pushed aside to make clearance for a small bowl of hearty tomato soup. Garnish with fresh basil.

For your centerpiece, keep grass growing in interesting low containers. For casual lunches or dinners, bring one out, give it a trim and make it the focus of your table.

Edie's Mushroom and Chicken Delight

- 2   8-ounce packages fresh mushrooms
- 2   cups cooked chopped chicken
- ½   cup Moore's Marinade™
- 1   medium clove garlic, minced
- 2   tablespoons green onions, finely chopped
- 2   tablespoons fresh basil, finely chopped
- ⅓   cup olive oil
- 2   teaspoons fresh jalapeno peppers, seeded and minced
- ⅓   cup fresh lemon juice
- 3   small strips of lemon rind, yellow portion only
- 2   tablespoons dry white wine
- ¼   cup plain, low-fat yogurt

Wipe the mushrooms with a clean, damp cloth, and cut into quarters. Set aside with chicken.

In a shallow bowl, combine the Moore's Marinade™ and remaining ingredients and mix well. Toss the mushrooms and chicken in the mixture to coat evenly. Cover and refrigerate, stirring occasionally, for several hours or overnight.

Remove the mushrooms and chicken from the marinade. Discard the marinade and serve cold. Serves 4.

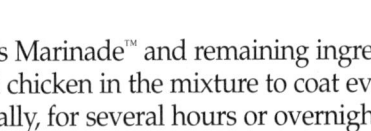

Nutritional Information

Information per serving (4 servings)

Calories	236	Percentage of Calories from Carbohydrates: 12%
Carbohydrates	7 gm	Percentage of Calories from Protein: 42%
Protein	25 gm	Percentage of Calories from Fat: 46%
Fat	12 gm	
Cholesterol	60 mg	Diabetic Food Exchange
Sodium	35 mg	Carbohydrate: 0.5
Fiber	1 gm	Protein: 3.5
Calcium	35 mg	Fat: 2.5
Iron	2 mg	
Vitamin A	99 IU	
Vitamin C	12 mg	

Real Style

Although served cold, with fresh jalapeno peppers this dish warms the palate. The cooked chicken makes a substantial meal in warm or freezing weather.

The styling is simple: place chicken and mushrooms on a bed of lettuce, using individual dinner plates. Add a warm loaf of bread, and a mug of soup. For your centerpiece, place a sliced loaf of bread in a basket with a colored napkin under it. Pair this with a dish, small basket, or clay pot of raw mushrooms. Use similarly colored paper or cloth napkins at each place setting. Guests can place sliced bread directly on their dinner plates or, if you prefer, use bread and butter plates.

Microwave Ham Casserole

- 1⅓ cups cooked rice
- 1 medium onion, chopped
- 1 can cream of celery soup
- 1 8-ounce can pineapple chunks, with juice
- ¼ cup water
- 1 teaspoon brown sugar
- ½ pound lean baked or boiled ham, sliced
  sliced green onions, for garnish (optional)

Cook the rice according to package directions. Spread the rice in a casserole dish and set aside. Place chopped onion in a microwave-safe, covered bowl and microwave on high until tender, about 1 minute. Add the soup, pineapple with juice, water, and brown sugar to the onion. Heat covered on high until the mixture begins to boil, about 1 minute. Stir mixture until the brown sugar is dissolved.

Pour half the soup mixture over the rice. Arrange the ham slices on top of the rice and pour the remaining soup mixture over the ham. Cover loosely with plastic wrap or a paper towel (to prevent splatters in the microwave) and heat on high until the rice is reheated and the ham is warm, about 1 minute. Serves 4.

Nutritional Information

Information per serving (4 servings)

Calories	361	Percentage of Calories from Carbohydrates: 69%
Carbohydrates	62 gm	Percentage of Calories from Protein: 19%
Protein	17 gm	Percentage of Calories from Fat: 12%
Fat	5 gm	
Cholesterol	43 mg	**DIABETIC EXCHANGE**
Sodium	358 mg	Carbohydrate: 4
Fiber	2 gm	Protein: 2.5
Calcium	45 mg	Fat: 1
Iron	3 mg	
Vitamin A	120 IU	(If you are on a sodium-restricted diet, consider
Vitamin C	11 mg	substituting chicken or turkey breast for the ham.)

Real Style

Place the casserole on a platter for serving. Use canned red crab apples to place on the platter around the casserole dish, alternating with parsley sprigs. This looks festive and these garnishes are delicious. Add a corn dish and a green vegetable to complete the meal.

Place three different heights of candlesticks on the center of the table with candles to enhance the ambiance of the dining experience.

Seafood Gumbo

2 cups fresh okra, sliced or one 10-ounce package of frozen okra, no salt added, sliced
¼ cup vegetable oil
⅔ cup green onions and tops, chopped
3 cloves garlic, finely chopped
½ teaspoon freshly ground black pepper
2 cups water
1 cup canned, no-salt-added tomatoes
2 fresh bay leaves
½ cup uncooked rice
1 tablespoon Moore's Marinade™
1 pound fresh medium shrimp, peeled and deveined
½ pound scallops
1 teaspoon hot pepper sauce

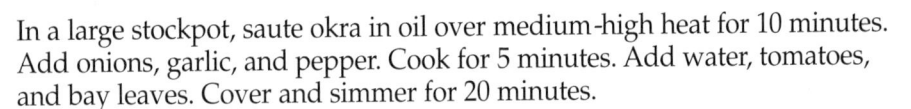

In a large stockpot, saute okra in oil over medium-high heat for 10 minutes. Add onions, garlic, and pepper. Cook for 5 minutes. Add water, tomatoes, and bay leaves. Cover and simmer for 20 minutes.

Meanwhile, cook rice with Moore's Marinade™ according to package directions. Do not use salt, butter, or margarine. Set aside.

Add shrimp and scallops to okra mixture. Cover and remove from heat. Let stand for 5 minutes, or until shrimp turns pink. Do not overcook.

Remove bay leaves and sprinkle with hot pepper sauce. Stir to mix well. Place ¼ cup of cooked rice in each soup bowl. Ladle equal amounts of gumbo over rice and serve hot. Serves 6.

Nutritional Information

Information per serving (6 servings)

Calories	287	Percentage of Calories from Carbohydrates: 28%
Carbohydrates	20 gm	Percentage of Calories from Protein: 38%
Protein	27 gm	Percentage of Calories from Fat: 34%
Fat	11 gm	
Cholesterol	114 mg	**DIABETIC EXCHANGES**
Sodium	196 mg	Carbohydrate: 1
Fiber	2 gm	Protein: 4
Calcium	95 mg	Fat: 2
Iron	3 mg	
Vitamin A	824 IU	
Vitamin C	15 mg	

Real Style

For your centerpiece, arrange colored Mardi Gras beads, a jester's hat, or a rendition of a Mardi Gras mask in the center of the table. They are colorful and lend to the festive atmosphere. Add confetti around centerpiece and all over table lightly before setting the table.

Spicy Chicken Chowder

1½ cups tomato juice or vegetable juice cocktail
3   tablespoons chopped onion
3   tablespoons chopped green pepper
2   tablespoons diced celery
⅓   cup diced potato
¼   teaspoon dried basil
2   cups cooked chicken breast, diced
1   teaspoon pepper

Combine first 5 ingredients in a small saucepan. Bring to a boil, reduce heat, and simmer until vegetables are tender, about 10 to 15 minutes. Add basil and diced chicken. Heat thoroughly. Taste and add seasoning as desired. Serves 2.

Nutritional Information

Information per serving (2 servings)

Calories	323	
Carbohydrates	19 gm	
Protein	55 gm	
Fat	3 gm	
Cholesterol	131 mg	
Sodium	816 mg	
Fiber	2 gm	
Calcium	56 mg	
Iron	3 mg	
Vitamin A	1166 IU	
Vitamin C	9 mg	

Percentage of Calories from Carbohydrates: 24%
Percentage of Calories from Protein: 68%
Percentage of Calories from Fat: 8%

DIABETIC EXCHANGES
Carbohydrate: 1
Protein: 7.5
Fat: 0.5

Real Style

Chowder as a meal or partnered with a tossed salad or rolls is filling and energizing. Prepare a casual setting with woven placemats, and simple bright plates and bowls. Use cubed green peppers and fresh ground pepper for garnish.

Your centerpiece consists of a stack of lemons placed on a painted pottery breakfast plate, pyramid style. Use boxwood sprigs [well washed] to fill in spaces. Place lemon wedges around the bottom of the stack.

Greek Burgers

- ½ pound ground lamb
- ½ pound ground beef or turkey
- 3 tablespoons chopped fresh parsley
- 2 tablespoons chopped fresh chives
- 1 tablespoon chopped fresh basil
- 1 garlic clove, minced
- ¼ teaspoon salt
- 1 teaspoon oregano
- ½ teaspoon chopped fresh or dried rosemary
- ½ teaspoon pepper
- 4 large crusty French rolls, split
- Toppings: lettuce, yellow tomato slices, purple onion slices

Combine all ingredients. Shape into 4 patties. Grill, with cover down, over medium-high heat for 5–6 minutes on each side or until meat is no longer pink.

Place desired toppings on the burger once it is on a roll. Serves 4.

Nutritional Information

Information per serving (4 servings)

Calories	343	Percentage of Calories from Carbohydrates: 22%
Carbohydrates	19 gm	Percentage of Calories from Protein: 39%
Protein	33 gm	Percentage of Calories from Fat: 39%
Fat	15 gm	
Cholesterol	85 mg	DIABETIC EXCHANGES
Sodium	459 mg	Carbohydrate: 1
Fiber	1 gm	Protein: 4.5
Calcium	57 mg	Fat: 3
Iron	3 mg	
Vitamin A	265 IU	
Vitamin C	5 mg	(Note: Does not include toppings)

Real Style

This Greek dish is easy to prepare. Let your condiments be the centerpiece for this meal: a large platter of iceberg and curly lettuce, tomatoes, onions, cheese slices, and pickles. Arrange in an attractive way. You may add other visually appealing items, such as green or ripe olives, radishes, or a variety of bell peppers.

Serve with grilled potato wedges. Brush potato wedges with a flavored oil before grilling with burgers.

Poached Salmon

4 thick salmon steaks (about 4 ounces each)
1 cup chicken stock
1 cup white wine
1 bay leaf
1 teaspoon tarragon
1 cup chopped green onions
crushed pepper to taste
fresh dill
lemon wedges

Put salmon in deep skillet.

Combine remaining ingredients and pour over salmon. Cover and simmer gently 10–15 minutes.

Sprinkle with dill and serve with lemon wedges. 4 servings.

Nutritional Information

Information per serving (4 servings)

Calories	218	Percentage of Calories from Carbohydrates: 8%
Carbohydrates	4 gm	Percentage of Calories from Protein: 51%
Protein	28 gm	Percentage of Calories from Fat: 41%
Fat	10 gm	
Cholesterol	46 mg	DIABETIC EXCHANGES
Sodium	585 mg	Carbohydrate: 0.5
Fiber	0 gm	Protein: 4
Calcium	40 mg	Fat: 2
Iron	1 mg	
Vitamin A	2233 IU	
Vitamin C	4 mg	

Real Style

To create a visually lovely meal with this entree, complete this dish with fresh asparagus, hollandaise or Bearnaise sauce, and rice, if desired. This will make a beautiful combination on the plate. Add a glass of your favorite white wine or sparkling white grape juice. Loosely tie a cloth napkin around the neck of your bottle for serving. Choose a couple of crystal or clear candlesticks with candles and a small vase with one, three, or five flowers in it, for balance and interest.

Country-Style Chicken Kiev

- ⅔ cup sweet cream butter or I Can't Believe It's Not Butter™
- ½ cup fine dry breadcrumbs
- 2 tablespoons grated Parmesan cheese
- ½ teaspoon basil
- ½ teaspoon oregano
- ½ teaspoon garlic salt
- 2 large boneless chicken breasts, split with skin removed, about 1 pound
- ¼ cup dry white wine (or apple juice)
- ¼ cup chopped onion
- ¼ cup chopped parsley

Preheat oven to 375°F.

Melt butter in heavy, 2-quart saucepan.

Meanwhile, on a piece of wax paper (or in plastic bag), combine breadcrumbs, cheese, and spices together well. Dip chicken in melted butter, then roll in crumb mixture, coating both sides.

Place chicken in a 9-inch square baking dish. Bake in the center of the oven for 50–60 minutes or until golden brown.

Meanwhile, add wine, onion, and parsley to remaining butter in saucepan, and bring to simmer.

Remove chicken from oven, pour butter-wine mixture over chicken, and return to oven for 3–5 minutes. Serves 4.

Nutritional Information

Information per serving (4 servings)

Calories	363	
Carbohydrates	11 gm	
Protein	28 gm	
Fat	23 gm	
Cholesterol	126 mg	
Sodium	619 mg	
Fiber	0 gm	
Calcium	107 mg	
Iron	2 mg	
Vitamin A	1037 IU	
Vitamin C	7 mg	

Percentage of Calories from Carbohydrates: 12%
Percentage of Calories from Protein: 31%
Percentage of Calories from Fat: 57%

DIABETIC EXCHANGES
Carbohydrate: 1
Protein: 4
Fat: 5

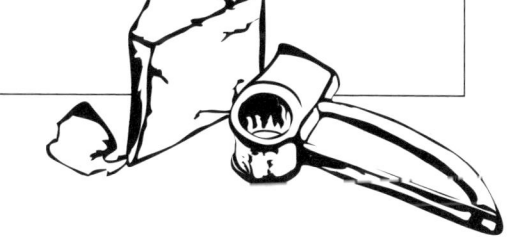

Chicken a la King

1. can low-fat golden cream of mushroom soup
1. can low-fat cream of chicken soup
1. 6-ounce can of evaporated milk
1. 4-ounce can of mushrooms or 4 ounces of chopped mushrooms
½ cup toasted almonds
1. teaspoon white pepper
½ cup green pepper, chopped
¼ cup pimentos, chopped
1½ cups chicken, chopped
3. cups chow mein noodles or puff pastry cups

Preheat oven to 350°F.

Combine all ingredients except noodles/puff pastry cups in a 2-quart casserole, mixing well.

Bake for 1 hour and serve over noodles or puff pastry cups. Great for a bridal shower or luncheon. Serves 4.

Nutritional Information

Information per serving (4 servings)

Calories	335	
Carbohydrates	25 gm	
Protein	25 gm	
Fat	15 gm	
Cholesterol	51 mg	
Sodium	935 mg	
Fiber	1 gm	
Calcium	125 mg	
Iron	2 mg	
Vitamin A	666 IU	
Vitamin C	20 mg	

Percentage of Calories from Carbohydrates: 30%
Percentage of Calories from Protein: 30%
Percentage of Calories from Fat: 40%

DIABETIC EXCHANGES
Carbohydrate: 2
Protein: 3
Fat: 3

Real Style

To make an attractive presentation, fully open the napkins. Pick up the center of each napkin with your index finger and thumb, and let sides fall in place. Tie a loose bow around napkin center using fabric ribbon, tulle, twine, or other easily accessible items. Place napkin on plate. Serve chicken with a mixed green salad.

For your centerpiece, gather any greenery you may have growing in a variety of sizes. Using a pitcher, arrange the tall greenery on the inside middle, and medium and small pieces around the edges. You can add flowers to greenery if desired.

Irresistible Pork Chops

4 ½-inch, center-cut pork chops, 4 ounces each
½ **cup low-fat mayonnaise**
1½ cups Italian-seasoned bread crumbs

Preheat oven to 425°F.

Brush pork chops on all sides with mayonnaise. Place breadcrumbs in large plastic bag. Add pork chops one piece at a time, and shake to coat well.

Place on rack in broiler pan. Bake 40 minutes or until golden brown and tender.

Can also be made with fish or chicken. Serves 4.

Nutritional Information

Information per serving (4 servings)

Calories	380	
Carbohydrates	34 gm	
Protein	25 gm	
Fat	16 gm	
Cholesterol	59 mg	
Sodium	1471 mg	
Fiber	2 gm	
Calcium	50 mg	
Iron	2 mg	
Vitamin A	66 IU	
Vitamin C	0 mg	

Percentage of Calories from Carbohydrates: 36%
Percentage of Calories from Protein: 26%
Percentage of Calories from Fat: 38%

DIABETIC EXCHANGES
Carbohydrate: 2
Protein: 3
Fat: 3

Real Style

For your centerpiece, use a live plant. If the plant is in a clay pot, transplant it into a beautiful glass, china, or stonewear bowl, just for the meal. Use red, canned crab apples for a garnish if desired.

Kids Tip

Let children help brush mayonnaise on the pork chops and shake them in the plastic food bags. This is not only fun, it is a bonding moment and encourages kids to eat. Also ask your children what they would like with the pork chops. Make suggestions like low-sugar applesauce or reduced-fat macaroni and cheese.

Asparagus-Chicken Parmesan

25–30 fresh steamed or frozen asparagus spears
1   pound chicken, cooked and diced
1   cup Parmesan cheese, freshly grated
1   cup low-fat mayonnaise
½   teaspoon salt
¼   cup lemon juice
¾   cup sliced almonds, toasted

Preheat oven to 350°F.

Cook asparagus until tender. Drain well.

Layer asparagus and chicken in a lightly greased 12x8x2-inch baking dish. Combine next 4 ingredients, mixing well. Spoon mixture over chicken and asparagus. Sprinkle top with toasted almonds.

Bake for 20–25 minutes or until heated thoroughly. Serves 4.

Nutritional Information

Information per serving (4 servings)

Calories	369	Percentage of Calories from Carbohydrates: 9%
Carbohydrates	8 gm	Percentage of Calories from Protein: 30%
Protein	28 gm	Percentage of Calories from Fat: 61%
Fat	25 gm	
Cholesterol	71 mg	DIABETIC EXCHANGES
Sodium	875 mg	Carbohydrate: 0.5
Fiber	2 gm	Protein: 4
Calcium	275 mg	Fat: 5
Iron	2 mg	
Vitamin A	340 IU	
Vitamin C	9 mg	

Real Style

Sliced tomatoes fanned out on a lettuce leaf will look great on a luncheon or dinner plate. Place a very small amount of mayonnaise on tomatoes. Sprinkle with paprika.

Create a fresh vegetable centerpiece using a medium clay saucer, and place a bunch of standing fresh asparagus, loosely tied in the center with red or orange raffia. Choose grape or cherry tomatoes to place around bottom of asparagus. If available, choose five to seven unshelled almonds to add to the tomatoes. Add white, orange, red, or green napkins and placemats on a white or ecru tablecloth.

Eggplant Parmesan

This recipe is courtesy of Melissa Donaldson, RD, LD, Heart College at HealthSouth

- 1 small onion, finely chopped
- 2 cloves garlic, minced
- ¾ cup extra-virgin olive oil
- 1 28-ounce can diced tomatoes
- 2 medium firm and fresh eggplants (about 1 pound each)
- ½ cup flour
- 2 large eggs, slightly beaten
- 1 cup dried breadcrumbs, flavor of choice, wholegrain preferable
- 1 pound part-skim mozzarella cheese, thinly sliced
- 1 cup freshly grated Parmesan cheese
- 1 tablespoon chopped fresh Italian (flat-leaf) parsley

Preheat oven to 400°F.

In a medium skillet over medium heat, saute the onion and garlic in ¼ cup of the olive oil until the onion is translucent but not brown. Add the diced tomatoes and stir to combine. Simmer gently 15 to 20 minutes, until the sauce thickens slightly. Remove from heat.

Meanwhile, wash and slice the eggplant into thin slices, ¼-inch thick at most.

Nutritional Information

Information per serving (6 servings)

Calories	346	Percentage of Calories from Carbohydrates: 35%
Carbohydrates	30 gm	Percentage of Calories from Protein: 18%
Protein	16 gm	Percentage of Calories from Fat: 47%
Fat	18 gm	
Cholesterol	82 mg	DIABETIC EXCHANGES
Sodium	534 mg	Carbohydrate: 2
Fiber	4 gm	Protein: 2
Calcium	351 mg	Fat: 3.5
Iron	2 mg	
Vitamin A	1012 IU	Note: for a lower-fat variation, use only ⅓ cup of olive oil, ½ pound of mozzarella cheese, and ½ cup of Parmesan cheese.
Vitamin C	18 mg	

(You can peel the eggplants if preferred, but it is not necessary.) Dip the eggplant slices in the flour, then into the egg mixture, then into the breadcrumbs to coat.

In a large skillet, heat the remaining ½ cup olive oil until a breadcrumb sizzles on contact. Fry the eggplant slices quickly and carefully until tender, adding more oil if necessary. Drain on paper towels on a wire rack and salt lightly.

Coat a 9x13-inch baking pan with ½ cup of the tomato sauce. Layer the remaining ingredients as follows: One third of the eggplant slices, one third of the remaining sauce, half the mozzarella slices, one third of the eggplant slices, one third of the sauce, half the grated Parmesan cheese, then the remaining eggplant, sauce, mozzarella, and Parmesan. Top with the chopped parsley. Bake 40 minutes, remove from the oven and allow to sit for at least 15 minutes before serving. Serves 6.

Chicken Breasts with Swiss Cheese

- 6 boneless chicken breasts, 6 ounces each
- 2 cans low-fat cream of mushroom soup
- 1 18-ounce package Pepperidge Farm™ herb stuffing
- ½ pound melted butter or I Can't believe It's Not Butter™
- ½ pound low-fat Swiss cheese

Preheat oven to 425°F.

Place chicken breasts in greased 9x13-inch pan.

Top each breast with one slice of Swiss cheese, pour soup over top, cover with stuffing, and drizzle with melted butter or margarine.

Cook uncovered for 30 minutes. Serves 6.

Nutritional Information

Information per serving (6 servings)

Calories	740	
Carbohydrates	25 gm	
Protein	52 gm	
Fat	48 gm	
Cholesterol	168 mg	
Sodium	1951 mg	
Fiber	3 gm	
Calcium	353 mg	
Iron	3 mg	
Vitamin A	1989 IU	
Vitamin C	3 mg	

Percentage of Calories from Carbohydrates: 14%
Percentage of Calories from Protein: 28%
Percentage of Calories from Fat: 58%

DIABETIC EXCHANGES
Carbohydrate: 2
Protein: 7.5
Fat: 10

Note: To lower the fat and sodium content, use less cheese and see food exchanges starting on page 94.

Real Style

Turn your cloth dinner napkins into placemats. Let them hang about three inches over the edge of the table at each place setting. Roll up another cloth or paper napkin; place it in a napkin ring and position above the dinner plate. Choose a color theme that reflects your china or earthenware and paint a large tin in the same shades. Use three varieties of fresh flowers from the floral department of your supermarket, your garden, or florist.

Chicken Tenders

- ¾ cup breadcrumbs
- ½ cup Parmesan cheese
- 4½ tablespoons minced parsley
- ¾ tablespoon salt
- ¼ tablespoon pepper
- 1½ cups margarine or butter, melted
- 3 tablespoons lemon juice
- 2 cloves garlic, crushed
- 6 boneless chicken breasts, about 6 ounces each, cut into strips
- 1 teaspoon paprika

Preheat oven to 350°F.

In a bowl, combine breadcrumbs, Parmesan cheese, parsley, and salt and pepper to taste.

In another bowl combine butter, lemon juice, and crushed garlic.

Dip chicken in butter mixture, then cover in crumbs. Place in casserole dish and drizzle with remaining butter and paprika.

Bake for 35 minutes. Serves 6.

Nutritional Information

Information per serving (6 servings)

Calories	352	Percentage of Calories from Carbohydrates: 4%
Carbohydrates	4 gm	Percentage of Calories from Protein: 55%
Protein	48 gm	Percentage of Calories from Fat: 41%
Fat	16 gm	
Cholesterol	24 mg	DIABETIC EXCHANGES
Sodium	753 mg	Carbohydrate: 0.5
Fiber	0 gm	Protein: 7
Calcium	36 mg	Fat: 3
Iron	0 mg	
Vitamin A	753 IU	
Vitamin C	2 mg	

Real Style

Use vibrant red placemats and white napkins with simple white china. Small clay pots holding geraniums or primroses create cheerful centerpieces. Wrap and swag pots with colorful fabric and raffia for a nice touch.

Herb and Lemon Fried Chicken

- ⅓ cup olive oil
- 3 cloves of garlic, chopped
- 2 lemons
- 2 tablespoons fresh rosemary
- 2 tablespoons ground pepper
- 2 chickens cut into pieces (4 each of thighs, breasts, legs, and wings)
- 1½ cups flour
- 1 teaspoon salt
- ¼ cup chopped basil
- ¼ cup chopped rosemary
- 1 egg
- ¾ cup milk
- safflower or peanut oil
- lemon slices

Combine the olive oil, coarsely chopped garlic, juice of one lemon and its grated rind, rosemary, pepper, and chicken pieces in a pan or large bowl.

Make sure all the chicken pieces are well coated with the marinade. Refrigerate overnight or for at least 5 hours.

Mix the flour, salt, and herbs together in a large bowl. Mix egg and milk in a separate bowl. Dredge chicken in egg mixture, then flour mixture.

Fill heavy, large frying pan with about 1 inch of oil and heat over medium-high eat until very hot.

Fry the chicken in batches (do not overcrowd the pan). Cook 12 minutes, about 6 minutes each side. Lower heat if chicken is browning too quickly. Drain on paper towels.

Thin lemon slices can be breaded and fried in the oven or served on the side to squirt juice on cooked chicken. Serves 6.

Nutritional Information

Information per serving (6 servings)

Calories	467	Percentage of Calories from Carbohydrates: 26%
Carbohydrates	30 gm	Percentage of Calories from Protein: 45%
Protein	53 gm	Percentage of Calories from Fat: 29%
Fat	15 gm	
Cholesterol	88 mg	DIABETIC EXCHANGES
Sodium	1160 mg	Carbohydrate: 2
Fiber	3 gm	Protein: 7.5
Calcium	82 mg	Fat: 3
Iron	3 mg	
Vitamin A	285 IU	
Vitamin C	13 mg	

Lemon Chicken

- 2 2-pound chickens, cut into serving-size portions (or 16 thighs), skin left on
- 2 tablespoons butter
- 2 tablespoons olive oil
- 6 large lemons
- 1½ teaspoons salt
- ½ teaspoon pepper
- 2 tablespoons garlic powder
- 2 tablespoons oregano

Preheat oven to 350°F.

Heat butter and olive oil over medium heat in a large heavy skillet, add all chicken pieces and brown them slowly for 10 minutes, turning after 5 minutes.

Place chicken pieces very close together in an 8x10-inch baking pan. Pour remaining butter and olive oil mixture over chicken. Cut four of the lemons into quarters, and squeeze a few over chicken, then place empty rinds around the chicken. Sprinkle all spices over the chicken.

Cook for 30–40 minutes or until chicken is done. Every 15 minutes, squeeze lemon juice over chicken. Serve with lemon wedges. Serves 8.

Nutritional Information

Information per serving (8 servings)

Calories	404	Percentage of Calories from Carbohydrates: 8%
Carbohydrates	8 gm	Percentage of Calories from Protein: 48%
Protein	48 gm	Percentage of Calories from Fat: 44%
Fat	20 gm	
Cholesterol	261 mg	DIABETIC EXCHANGES
Sodium	890 mg	Carbohydrate: 0.5
Fiber	2 gm	Protein: 7
Calcium	73 mg	Fat: 4
Iron	4 mg	
Vitamin A	461 IU	
Vitamin C	41 mg	

Real Style

Give family and friends a pleasing aroma straight from your centerpiece by using lemons. Make a lemon tree on a dinner plate, breakfast plate, or medium clay saucer, (clay saucers can be painted to match decor), three to five tiers high. Use toothpicks to hold lemons in place, preferably not seen. Add sprig of greenery or parsley in spaces. Use yellow, white, or green accessories.

Dijon Fish

- 4   8-ounce fish fillets
- 1   tablespoon vegetable oil
- 1   clove garlic
- 1   tablespoon butter
- 1½ cups soft Italian or French breadcrumbs
-     chopped parsley
- ½   teaspoon pepper
- 1   egg
- 1   tablespoon water
- ½   cup half & half
- 1   teaspoon Dijon-style mustard
- 8   ounces white wine
- 1 teaspoon flour to thicken

(This recipe is also delicious using pork chops or chicken breasts)

Preheat oven to 400°F.

In a large skillet, brown fish on both sides in oil; remove and set aside in small pan.

Saute garlic in butter. Stir in breadcrumbs, parsley, and pepper; set aside.

Combine egg and water. Dip fish into egg mixture, then into breadcrumb mixture. Place fish on a well-greased baking sheet. Bake for 12–15 minutes or until cooked through.

Meanwhile, pour excess fat from skillet; add half & half and heat while stirring. Stir in mustard, white wine, and flour, continuing to stir until thickened. Serve fish with sauce. Serves 4.

Nutritional Information

Information per serving (4 servings)

Calories	507	Percentage of Calories from Carbohydrates: 29%
Carbohydrates	37 gm	Percentage of Calories from Protein: 44%
Protein	56 gm	Percentage of Calories from Fat: 27%
Fat	15 gm	
Cholesterol	106 mg	DIABETIC EXCHANGES
Sodium	1130 mg	Carbohydrate: 2.5
Fiber	2 gm	Protein: 8
Calcium	90 mg	Fat: 3
Iron	2 mg	
Vitamin A	407 IU	
Vitamin C	1 mg	

Real Style

Us three small containers of flowers and clusters of cathedral candles (five), to lend a more formal table setting or serve buffet-style from the dining room sideboard. Candles lend a relaxed yet elegant atmosphere and an openhearted air.

Asian Beef

- 7 ounces lean round steak (¼-inch thick)
- 1 teaspoon cornstarch
- 1 teaspoon ground ginger (pinch)
- 2 tablespoons low-sodium soy sauce
- 1 small green pepper (2¼ inches in diameter), cut into ½-inch squares
- ½ cup diced onion
- ¼ cup sliced carrots
- 3 tablespoons water
- 1 garlic clove, minced
- 1 tomato, cut into 1-inch cubes

Place steak briefly in freezer until firm to make slicing easier. Slice steak diagonally, across the grain, into strips as thin as possible.

Combine cornstarch, ginger, and soy sauce in a small bowl. Add meat and toss to coat each slice.

Coat a nonstick skillet with vegetable cooking spray.

Heat skillet over medium-high heat. Add meat and brown quickly, set aside.

Add peppers, onion, carrots, water, and garlic to skillet and, stirring constantly, cook for 5–6 minutes until carrots and peppers are tender-crisp. Stir in meat and tomato. Heat thoroughly. Serves 2.

Nutritional Information

Information per serving (2 servings)

Calories	234	
Carbohydrates	12 gm	
Protein	24 gm	
Fat	10 gm	
Cholesterol	55 mg	
Sodium	616 mg	
Fiber	2 gm	
Calcium	26 mg	
Iron	3 mg	
Vitamin A	5803 IU	
Vitamin C	77 mg	

Percentage of Calories from Carbohydrates: 21%
Percentage of Calories from Protein: 41%
Percentage of Calories from Fat: 38%

DIABETIC EXCHANGES
Carbohydrate: 1
Protein: 3
Fat: 2

Real Style

Use the Asian theme for table decorations. Sew or glue a band of fabric similar to napkins around an inexpensive woven natural beach mat to use for a table runner.

Use sticks of bamboo available in garden shops or greens growing in your yard. Cut bamboo into varying lengths, attach with hot glue to sides of two, six-inch pillar candles and tie with thin cord. Place candles in the center of the runner.

Prime Rib Roast with Garlic

1 4-pound rib roast
10 cloves garlic, peeled
   Salt and pepper to taste

Preheat oven to 500°F.

Slice garlic cloves in half lengthwise. With a sharp paring knife pierce roast to a depth of 1–2 inches and insert garlic evenly spaced on top. Lightly salt and pepper the entire roast.

Place in broiler pan and set on middle rack of oven. Roast for 15 minutes. Turn oven down to 325°F and continue to roast for 18 minutes per pound for medium–rare beef.

Remove from oven, cover with foil, and let stand 15 minutes before serving. To serve, slice roast into ¼-inch slices. Place on warm platter. Serves 8.

Nutritional Information

Information per serving (8 servings)

Calories	339	
Carbohydrates	1 gm	
Protein	50 gm	
Fat	15 gm	
Cholesterol	125 mg	
Sodium	103 mg	
Fiber	0 gm	
Calcium	18 mg	
Iron	2 mg	
Vitamin A	14 IU	
Vitamin C	2 mg	

Percentage of Calories from Carbohydrates: 1%
Percentage of Calories from Protein: 59%
Percentage of Calories from Fat: 40%

DIABETIC EXCHANGES
Carbohydrate: 0
Protein: 7
Fat: 3

Real Style

It's easy to make this an eye-catching dish. Just place partially sliced roast on warmed platter. Use canned red crab apples and parsley alternating around roast. Add colorful veggies in attractive serving dishes. A tossed green or fruit salad served in separate bowls or on salad plates will make this meal more formal. Place tall candlesticks with dripless candles in center of table, leaving spaces so guests can enjoy conversing across the table.

Sirloin Burgers

- 1 pound lean ground sirloin
- 1 clove garlic, minced
- ½ cup feta cheese, crumbled (about 2 ounces)
- ⅓ cup pitted Kalamata olives, minced
- ½ teaspoon salt, preferably kosher
- 6 medium-size pita breads, thick variety
- ¼ cup fruity olive oil, preferably extra virgin
- 1 teaspoon ground cumin mixed with 1 teaspoon ground coriander
  Vegetable oil for brushing on grill rack (optional for non-stick)
  tomato slices
  thin red onion slices
  red leaf lettuce

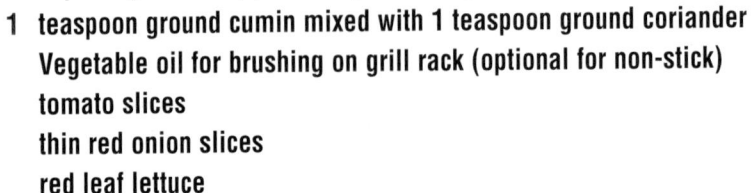

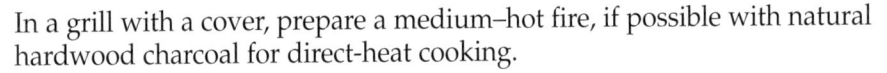

In a grill with a cover, prepare a medium–hot fire, if possible with natural hardwood charcoal for direct-heat cooking.

Combine the sirloin, garlic, cheese, olives, and salt in a large bowl.

Handling the meat as little as possible to avoid compacting it, mix well with ingredients in bowl. Divide the mixture into six equal portions and form the portions into round patties to fit the pita breads. Brush the patties with the olive oil and then sprinkle with the cumin mixture. Discard any unused olive oil.

When the fire is ready, brush the grill rack with vegetable oil. Place the patties on the grill, cover, and cook until browned on the bottom, about 4 minutes. With a wide spatula, turn the patties and cook until done to preference. During the last minute of cooking, place the pita breads on the outer edge of the grill and turn to toast lightly on both sides.

Offer the condiments at the table. Serves 6.

Nutritional Information

Information per serving (6 servings)

Calories	479	
Carbohydrates	37 gm	
Protein	22 gm	
Fat	27 gm	
Cholesterol	63 mg	
Sodium	792 mg	
Fiber	5 gm	
Calcium	89 mg	
Iron	4 mg	
Vitamin A	90 IU	
Vitamin C	0 mg	

Percentage of Calories from Carbohydrates: 31%
Percentage of Calories from Protein: 18%
Percentage of Calories from Fat: 51%

DIABETIC EXCHANGES
Carbohydrate: 2.5
Protein: 3
Fat: 5

Southern Meatloaf

- 1½ pounds ground sirloin
- ½ cup ketchup plus ¼ cup
- ½ cup tomato juice
- 2 eggs, beaten
- ½ cup fresh breadcrumbs
- ¼ cup minute oats
- ½ cup onion, finely chopped
- 2 teaspoons prepared mustard
- ¼ teaspoon salt
- ½ teaspoon pepper
- ¼ cup celery (optional)
- 2 tablespoons green pepper, finely chopped (optional)
- 1 tablespoon Moore's Marinade™

Preheat oven to 350°F.

Mix all ingredients together with hands and put in a baking dish.

Bake for about 1 hour (or until desired doneness). After baking for 45 minutes, pour additional ketchup on top and continue to bake. Serves 6.

Nutritional Information

Information per serving (6 servings)

Calories	374	Percentage of Calories from Carbohydrates: 19%
Carbohydrates	18 gm	Percentage of Calories from Protein: 28%
Protein	26 gm	Percentage of Calories from Fat: 53%
Fat	22 gm	
Cholesterol	160 mg	DIABETIC EXCHANGES
Sodium	760 mg	Carbohydrate: 1
Fiber	1 gm	Protein: 4
Calcium	59 mg	Fat: 4
Iron	4 mg	
Vitamin A	441 IU	
Vitamin C	8 mg	

Real Style

Experiment with a variety of containers for your fresh flowers. Try a champagne bucket, a silver teapot, egg-cups, or porcelain tumblers. Each can stand in as vases. Make every guest a star. Take an instant photo of each guest as they arrive and set the photos above each place setting for place cards. Use a creamy white cloth and soft colors in napkins to match your china.

Kids Tip

Use hands to mix ingredients together. Little hands may be perfect for this chore and create a fun memory in the kitchen for a young helper.

Moore's Marinade™ Mushrooms

- 1 8-ounce package of fresh Portabella mushrooms
- 8 ounces beef strips, slightly seared before marinating
- 1 cup red and green peppers, cut into strips
- ½ cup Moore's Marinade™
- ¼ cup I Can't Believe it's Not Butter™
- 1 teaspoon garlic salt
- 1 teaspoon pepper
- 1 teaspoon salt

Wipe off mushrooms and cut off ends.

Marinate mushrooms, beef, and peppers in Moore's Marinade™. Let sit for at least 15 minutes.

In a cast iron skillet, melt butter and add the mushrooms, beef, peppers, and remaining ingredients. Cook over medium heat, stirring frequently until mushrooms are very brown, 10–12 minutes. Serves 4.

Real Style
Using large washed and oiled terracotta saucers, cut a round of wax paper and place in the bottom of the saucer. Use a one-half-cup size clay pot and place in the center

Nutritional Information

Information per serving (4 servings)

Calories	202	
Carbohydrates	4 gm	
Protein	15 gm	
Fat	14 gm	
Cholesterol	26 mg	
Sodium	607 mg	
Fiber	1 gm	
Calcium	11 mg	
Iron	1 mg	
Vitamin A	520 IU	
Vitamin C	17 mg	

Percentage of Calories from Carbohydrates: 8%
Percentage of Calories from Protein: 30%
Percentage of Calories from Fat: 62%

DIABETIC EXCHANGES
Carbohydrate: 0.5
Protein: 2
Fat: 3

of the saucer for holding toothpicks. Place mushrooms, beef tips, and red and green peppers directly on the wax paper surrounding the small pot. Gather fall or green leaves, preferably oak, to scatter on the table from the centerpiece with a few around the mushroom dish.

The centerpiece consists of three bricks or small boxes for stepping heights. Choose three clay pots in three graduated sizes. Place the largest pot directly on the center of the table, the medium pot on one brick, and the smallest pot on two bricks. Place fresh mushrooms in medium pot, filled to overflow. Place flowers, fresh or dried, in the top small pot, and in the largest pot place rolled napkins for guests. Napkins can be paper or cloth, and placed in pot so they stand straight up. For added color try using patterned print napkins in fall colors.

Shrimp Pecan Vegetable Pilau

- 1½ pounds boiled, peeled, deveined shrimp
- ¼ cup Moore's Marinade™
- 1 medium onion
- 2 yellow squashes
- 1 carrot
- 2 cups fresh broccoli flowerets
- 3 tablespoons olive oil
- ½ teaspoon salt
- ¼ teaspoon pepper
- 1 can chicken broth
- ¾ cup uncooked converted rice
- ¼ cup thinly sliced, fresh basil
- ½ cup shredded cheese
- 2 tablespoons chopped pecans

Place shrimp and Moore's Marinade™ in a bowl. Stir to coat shrimp.

Cut onion in half, then cut each half into thin slices. Coarsely chop squash and cut carrot into diagonal slices.

Saute vegetables in hot oil in large skillet over medium-high heat for 8 minutes or until tender. Sprinkle with salt and pepper, and remove from skillet.

Bring chicken broth to a boil in a skillet; stir in rice. Cover and cook, stirring occasionally, for 20 minutes or until liquid is absorbed and rice is tender.

Stir vegetables, basil, cheese, and pecans into rice. To serve, arrange rice on four dinner plates and divide shrimp equally and place on rice. Makes 4 servings.

For variety, use chopped cooked chicken, beef, or ham.

Nutritional Information

Information per serving (4 servings)

Calories	582	Percentage of Calories from Carbohydrates: 30%
Carbohydrates	43 gm	Percentage of Calories from Protein: 36%
Protein	53 gm	Percentage of Calories from Fat: 34%
Fat	22 gm	
Cholesterol	293 mg	DIABETIC EXCHANGES
Sodium	976 mg	Carbohydrate: 3
Fiber	5 gm	Protein: 7.5
Calcium	172 mg	Fat: 4
Iron	7 mg	
Vitamin A	2370 IU	
Vitamin C	66 mg	

For other uses for Moore's Marinade™, go to www.mooresmarinade.com.

Beer-Battered Fried Shrimp and Vegetables

- 1 pound unpeeled large fresh shrimp
- 2 green tomatoes
- 1 zucchini, sliced
- ½ pound small whole okra
- 1½ cups flour
- 1 teaspoon Cajun seasoning
- 1 12-ounce can beer
- 2 large eggs
- 1 48-ounce bottle Mazola™ corn oil
- salt to taste (optional)

Peel shrimp and remove veins, if desired.

Cut each tomato into 8 wedges, and cut zucchini into ¼-inch thick slices. Slice okra.

Whisk together flour, Cajun seasoning, and beer. Whisk in eggs. Dip shrimp and vegetables in batter. Pour oil in a Dutch oven, heat to 350°F.

Deep fry shrimp and okra in batches for 1 minute or until golden brown. Drain on paper towels, and keep warm.

Nutritional Information

Information per serving (4 servings)

Calories	856	Percentage of Calories from Carbohydrates: 22%
Carbohydrates	47 gm	Percentage of Calories from Protein: 15%
Protein	32 gm	Percentage of Calories from Fat: 63%
Fat	60 gm	
Cholesterol	172 mg	DIABETIC EXCHANGES
Sodium	215 mg	Carbohydrate: 3
Fiber	4 gm	Protein: 5
Calcium	133 mg	Fat: 12
Iron	6 mg	
Vitamin A	1190 IU	
Vitamin C	37 mg	

Deep fry tomatoes and zucchini in batches, 2 minutes or until golden brown. Sprinkle shrimp and vegetables with salt if desired. Serve immediately. Serves 4.

Real Style

Make a centerpiece of a flat basket of beautiful seashells. Put three to five votive candles around basket. Add wine and water glasses for white wine or sparkling grape juice and cold ice water. Add a tossed salad in a plate or bowl, and napkins with your best napkin rings. Place the napkins to the left of silverwear. You will shine with guests when coordinating centerpiece and entree.

Greek Eggplant, Tomato, and Feta Pizza

- **1** pint grape tomatoes, halved
- **½** cup fresh basil, shredded
- **2** garlic cloves, pressed
- **2** tablespoons balsamic vinegar
- **½** teaspoon pepper
- **1** pound eggplant, cut into slices
- **¼** cup Mazola™ canola oil
- **1** pizza crust, 10-inch
- **4** ounces feta cheese, crumbled

Preheat oven to 450°F.

Stir together the first 6 ingredients, set aside.

Cut eggplant crosswise into ½-inch-thick slices. Brush both sides evenly with oil, and place on an aluminum foil–lined baking sheet. Broil 2 minutes on each side or until lightly browned.

Arrange eggplant slices evenly on pizza crust; top with tomato mixture, and sprinkle with feta cheese. Bake for 8–10 minutes, or until thoroughly heated. Serve immediately. Serves 4.

Nutritional Information

Information per serving (4 servings)

Calories	492	
Carbohydrates	67 gm	
Protein	11 gm	
Fat	20 gm	
Cholesterol	25 mg	
Sodium	1069 mg	
Fiber	4 gm	
Calcium	191 mg	
Iron	3 mg	
Vitamin A	427 IU	
Vitamin C	9 mg	

Percentage of Calories from Carbohydrates: 54%
Percentage of Calories from Protein: 9%
Percentage of Calories from Fat: 37%

DIABETIC EXCHANGES
Carbohydrate: 4.5
Protein: 1.5
Fat: 4

Kid's Tip

Ideal to put in your child's lunch bag: From a sheet of paper, cut out the shape of an ice cream cone with a scoop of ice cream on top and write a note on it about a special after-school plan: "Afternoon treat will be ice cream for you and me. You're my heart."

Spaghetti with Marinara Sauce

- 8 ounces spaghetti
- 2 cups marinara sauce (see recipe, page 56)
- 4 ounces part-skim mozzarella cheese, grated
- 4 teaspoons grated Parmesan cheese

Preheat oven to 325°F.

Cook spaghetti al dente, according to package directions. Drain.

Grease a casserole dish with vegetable cooking spray. Add cooked spaghetti to dish, then add marinara sauce. Stir to coat spaghetti evenly with sauce.

Top with grated mozzarella. Bake until cheese bubbles and starts to brown, about 10–15 minutes. Remove from oven, sprinkle with Parmesan, and serve. Serves 4.

Nutritional Information

Information per serving (4 servings)

Calories	321	
Carbohydrates	53 gm	
Protein	7 gm	
Fat	9 gm	
Cholesterol	18 mg	
Sodium	690 mg	
Fiber	3 gm	
Calcium	249 mg	
Iron	3 mg	
Vitamin A	649 IU	
Vitamin C	10 mg	

Percentage of Calories from Carbohydrates: 66%
Percentage of Calories from Protein: 9%
Percentage of Calories from Fat: 25%

DIABETIC EXCHANGES
Carbohydrate: 3.5
Protein: 1
Fat: 2

Real Style

Serve this dish with style and salute Italy with red and white table decor. Centerpiece consists of quick, deep-fried thin spaghetti pasta, placed on paper towels and dried completely. Immediately roll in Italian seasonings. Stand pasta in colored or clear parfait glass. Pasta sticks are edible and make great conversation pieces.

Marinara Sauce

- 12 ounces canned tomato juice
- 10 ounces canned stewed tomatoes
- 1 teaspoon minced onion
- ¼ pound fresh mushrooms, sliced
- ½ sweet red pepper, chopped
- 1 medium green pepper, chopped
- ½ teaspoon dried Italian seasoning
- 1 teaspoon garlic powder (dash)
- 1 teaspoon salt, to taste
- 1 teaspoon pepper, to taste

Combine all ingredients in a heavy saucepan, and simmer uncovered for 45 minutes.

Divide leftover sauce into individual, 2-cup serving-size containers and freeze.

Thaw and use as needed. Makes 4 cups.

Nutritional Information
Information per ½ cup serving

Calories	68	
Carbohydrates	14 gm	
Protein	3 gm	
Fat	0 gm	
Cholesterol	0 mg	
Sodium	1055 mg	
Fiber	2 gm	
Calcium	43 mg	
Iron	2 mg	
Vitamin A	972 IU	
Vitamin C	110 mg	

Percentage of Calories from Carbohydrates: 80%
Percentage of Calories from Protein: 18%
Percentage of Calories from Fat: 2%

DIABETIC EXCHANGES
Carbohydrate: 1
Protein: 0.5
Fat: 0

Ginger Broiled Fish

- 4 ounces fillet of flounder (fresh or frozen)
- 1½ teaspoons honey
- 1 tablespoon vegetable oil
- ⅛ teaspoon ground ginger
- 1 tablespoon lime juice (fresh or bottled)
- pinch of salt, to taste

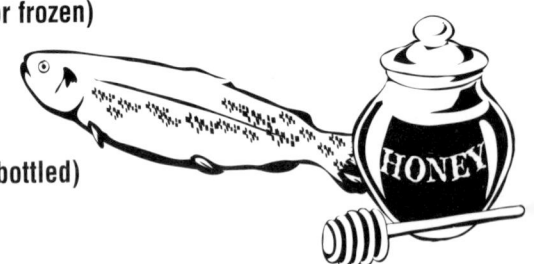

Thaw fish, if frozen. Place in shallow pan. Combine honey, oil, ginger, lime juice, and salt. Mix well and pour over fish.

Cover and chill for several hours, turning fish occasionally.

Pre-heat broiler. Remove fish from pan, reserving marinade.

Spray broiler with vegetable cooking spray. Arrange fillet so it is uniform in thickness. Broil 4 inches from heat until fish flakes easily when tested with a fork. Baste often with marinade. (Allow 5 minutes cooking time for each half inch of thickness. If fillet is thicker than 1 inch, turn halfway through cooking time). Brush with marinade just before serving. Serves 1.

Nutritional Information

Information per serving (1 serving)

Calories	283	
Carbohydrates	9 gm	
Protein	28 gm	
Fat	15 gm	
Cholesterol	54 mg	
Sodium	93 mg	
Fiber	0 gm	
Calcium	22 mg	
Iron	0 mg	
Vitamin A	38 IU	
Vitamin C	3 mg	

Percentage of Calories from Carbohydrates: 12%
Percentage of Calories from Protein: 40%
Percentage of Calories from Fat: 48%

DIABETIC EXCHANGES
Carbohydrate: 0.5
Protein: 4
Fat: 3

Real Style

This is an easy dinner for one. Make yourself feel special with this delight. Prepare wild, yellow, or white rice and a tossed salad. You deserve a flower, in a bud vase, and a lighted candle to honor yourself. Enjoy!

Roast Pork with Sweet Potato Treat

4–6 garlic cloves, minced
1 tablespoon fresh parsley, chopped, or 1 teaspoon dried parsley flakes
1 teaspoon coarse-ground black pepper
½ teaspoon dried thyme leaves
1 tablespoon lime or lemon juice
1 teaspoon olive oil
2 1-pound uncut pork tenderloins
4 sweet potatoes (medium size)
3 tablespoons honey
1 teaspoon cinnamon
1 cup pecan pieces

Preheat oven to 450°F.

Line a shallow roasting pan with foil, spray foil with nonstick cooking spray.

In a small bowl, combine garlic, parsley, pepper, and thyme. Stir lemon juice and olive oil together and pour mixture into a cup for basting convenience.

Brush pork with lemon juice mixture, coating well. Rub garlic-pepper mixture over top and sides of tenderloins, pressing lightly. Place in sprayed, foil-lined pan, garlic-pepper side up.

Bake for 25–35 minutes or until pork is no longer pink in center. Let stand for 5–10 minutes. Serve in diagonally cut half-inch slices. Serves 4.

For a Sweet Potato Treat With Your Pork Roast:
Bake sweet potatoes at 450°F for 50 minutes or until soft.

Remove from oven, slit potatoes down the middle. Pour in honey to taste over exposed part of potatoes. Sprinkle with cinnamon and pecan pieces. Return to oven for 3–5 minutes.

Nutritional Information

Information per serving of potato and pork (4 servings)

Calories	641	Percentage of Calories from Carbohydrates: 32%
Carbohydrates	51 gm	Percentage of Calories from Protein: 33%
Protein	53 gm	Percentage of Calories from Fat: 35%
Fat	25 gm	
Cholesterol	138 mg	DIABETIC EXCHANGES
Sodium	148 mg	Roast Pork / Sweet Potato Treat
Fiber	7 gm	Carbohydrate: 0 / Carbohydrate: 3
Calcium	106 mg	Protein: 7 / Protein: 0.5
Iron	4 mg	Fat: 3 / Fat: 2
Vitamin A	174 IU	
Vitamin C	35 mg	

Zucchini Sausage Bake

- 1 8-ounce package sweet Italian sausage
- 8 green onions, sliced (1 cup)
- 2 zucchini, diced (about 3 cups)
- 1 teaspoon salt
- ½ teaspoon pepper
- 1 7-ounce jar roasted red bell peppers, drained and chopped
- 1 16-ounce Italian bread loaf, cut into 1-inch cubes
- 2 cups (8 ounces) shredded sharp Cheddar cheese
- 6 large eggs
- 1½ cups milk

Remove and discard casing from sausage. Cook sausage in large skillet, stirring until sausage crumbles and is no longer pink; drain.

Add green onions and next 3 ingredients to skillet. Saute for 4 minutes or until vegetables are tender. Stir in roasted red peppers. Drain and cool.

Spread 4 cups of breadcrumbs in a lightly greased 13x9-inch baking dish. Top with half each of sausage mixture and cheese. Repeat with remaining bread, sausage, cheese.

Whisk together eggs and milk. Pour egg mixture over layers in baking dish. Cover and chill 8 hours. Bake at 325°F for 1 hour or until bubbly and hot. Serves 8.

Nutritional Information

Information per serving (8 servings)

Calories	470
Carbohydrates	35 gm
Protein	24 gm
Fat	26 gm
Cholesterol	241 mg
Sodium	1117 mg
Fiber	2 gm
Calcium	373 mg
Iron	3 mg
Vitamin A	2153 IU
Vitamin C	50 mg

Percentage of Calories from Carbohydrates: 30%
Percentage of Calories from Protein: 20%
Percentage of Calories from Fat: 50%

DIABETIC EXCHANGES
Carbohydrate: 2
Protein: 3
Fat: 5

Cornmeal Pancakes

- 1 cup white cornmeal
- 1 cup flour
- 1 teaspoon baking soda
- ½ teaspoon salt
- ½ teaspoon baking powder
- ½ cup sour cream
- 1 cup buttermilk
- 1 large egg, lightly beaten

Combine cornmeal and next 4 ingredients in a large bowl. Combine sour cream, buttermilk, and egg in a separate bowl; add to dry ingredients, stirring just until moistened.

Pour about 3 tablespoons of batter for each cake onto a hot, lightly greased griddle. Cook pancakes for 3 minutes or until top is covered in bubbles and edges look cooked.

Turn and cook for 2 more minutes. Cakes should be golden brown. Serve with honey or maple syrup. Serves 3.

Nutritional Information

Information per serving (3 servings)

Calories	456	Percentage of Calories from Carbohydrates: 64%
Carbohydrates	73 gm	Percentage of Calories from Protein: 12%
Protein	14 gm	Percentage of Calories from Fat: 24%
Fat	12 gm	
Cholesterol	102 mg	DIABETIC EXCHANGE
Sodium	1026 mg	Carbohydrate: 5
Fiber	4 gm	Protein: 2
Calcium	203 mg	Fat: 2
Iron	4 mg	
Vitamin A	452 IU	
Vitamin C	1 mg	

Real Style

Place brown burlap squares from fabric store around two, 16-ounce plastic cups or fruit jars. Tie burlap loosely with wrapping twine or natural or yellow-colored raffia. When using plastic or paper cups, place small stones in ⅓ of cup allowing room for water and floral stems. Fill cups with fresh daisies. Use yellow napkins with white dishes, paper or plastic products.

Seafood Bake

- 4 cups chicken broth
- ½ teaspoon salt (optional)
- 1 cup regular grits
- 1 cup (4 ounces) shredded sharp Cheddar cheese (¾ cup and ¼ cup)
- 1 cup (4 ounces) shredded Monterey Jack cheese, with peppers
- 2 tablespoons I Can't Believe It's Not Butter™
- 6 green onions, chopped
- 1 green bell pepper, chopped
- 1 garlic clove, minced
- ½ cup Moore's Marinade™
- 1 pound small fresh shrimp, peeled and cooked
- 1 10-ounce can diced tomatoes and green chilies, drained
- ¼ teaspoon pepper

Preheat oven to 350°F.

Bring chicken broth and salt to a boil in a large saucepan. Stir in grits. Cover, reduce heat, and simmer for 20 minutes.

Stir together grits, ¾ cup Cheddar cheese, and Monterey Jack cheese.

Melt butter in a large skillet over medium heat. Add green onions, bell pepper, and garlic. Saute with Moore's Marinade™ for 5 minutes or until tender.

Stir together green onion mixture, grits mixture, shrimp, and next 2 ingredients. Pour into a lightly greased, 2-quart baking dish. Sprinkle top with remaining ¼ cup shredded Cheddar cheese. Bake for 30–45 minutes. Serves 8.

Nutritional Information

Information per serving (8 servings)

Calories	233
Carbohydrates	9 gm
Protein	20 gm
Fat	13 gm
Cholesterol	114 mg
Sodium	1259 mg
Fiber	0 gm
Calcium	158 mg
Iron	2 mg
Vitamin A	776 IU
Vitamin C	21 mg

Percentage of Calories from Carbohydrates: 15%
Percentage of Calories from Protein: 35%
Percentage of Calories from Fat: 50%

DIABETIC EXCHANGE
Carbohydrate: 0.5
Protein: 3
Fat: 2.5

Quick and Easy Grits with Sausage Rolls

Sausage Roll
- 2–3 cups flour
- ¼ cup cooking oil
- 1 cup buttermilk
- 1 pound ground pork sausage

Preheat oven to 400°F.

Mix together first 3 ingredients. Pour onto a floured surface and knead. Roll dough out and crumble sausage onto it. Roll up jelly roll style, and slice. Bake 20 minutes or until golden brown.

Grits
- 2 cups boiling water
- 1⅓ cups instant grits
- 6 ounces shredded Cheddar cheese
- ¼ cup Parmesan cheese
- 2 eggs, beaten
- 2 tablespoons chives

Mix all ingredients and pour into a greased casserole dish. Bake at 350°F for 40 minutes. Serves 8.

Nutritional Information

Information per serving (8 servings)

Calories	438	
Carbohydrates	31 gm	
Protein	11 gm	
Fat	30 gm	
Cholesterol	39 mg	
Sodium	411 mg	
Fiber	1 gm	
Calcium	51 mg	
Iron	2 mg	
Vitamin A	10 IU	
Vitamin C	1 mg	

Percentage of Calories from Carbohydrates: 28%
Percentage of Calories from Protein: 10%
Percentage of Calories from Fat: 62%

DIABETIC EXCHANGES
Carbohydrate: 2
Protein: 1.5
Fat: 6

Real Style

Let your entree be your centerpiece by placing cut, baked sausage roll slices in an interesting large, low, rectangular basket. First, place an empty pickle jar in one end of basket. Lay a small tea towel folded flat in the portion of basket left. Place colored paper or cloth napkin over tea towel for rolls. Then arrange the roll neatly on the napkin. Fill jar with greenery or seasonal flowers.

Healthy Way Omelet

- 1 cup chopped onions
- ½ cup chopped green bell pepper
- 2 cloves garlic, minced
- 1 cup finely chopped fresh basil
- 1 tablespoon freshly chopped oregano
- 1 cup chopped fresh tomato
- 5 whole eggs
- 6 egg whites or ¾ cup cholesterol-free egg substitute
- ¼ cup skim milk
- ½ teaspoon salt
- ⅛ teaspoon black pepper
- 4 slices Italian bread
- 2 cloves garlic halved

Spray 12-inch skillet with non-stick cooking spray; heat over medium heat. Saute the first 6 ingredients together until tender; remove and set aside.

Beat whole eggs, egg whites, milk, salt, and pepper in a large bowl until foamy.

Pour egg mixture into skillet; cook over medium-high heat 2 to 3 minutes or until bottom of omelet is set. Reduce heat to medium-low. Cover, cook 8 minutes or until top of omelet is set; remove from heat.

Spoon vegetable mixture over the center of the omelet, fold over, let set.

Toast bread, rub both sides with garlic. Serve with omelet. Makes 4 servings.

Nutritional Information

Information per serving (4 servings)

Calories	230	Percentage of Calories from Carbohydrates: 42%
Carbohydrates	24 gm	Percentage of Calories from Protein: 35%
Protein	20 gm	Percentage of Calories from Fat: 23%
Fat	6 gm	
Cholesterol	205 mg	DIABETIC EXCHANGES
Sodium	371 mg	Carbohydrate: 1.5
Fiber	4 gm	Protein: 3
Calcium	98 mg	Fat: 1
Iron	2 mg	
Vitamin A	847 IU	
Vitamin C	24 mg	

Real Style

Cut a gallon milk jug in half, and set in the middle of a large printed cloth or paper dinner napkin. Bring napkin up around jug, creating a container. Stuff napkin ends inside of jug, using tape if necessary to secure. Place one medium potted blooming plant inside container. Use relaxed woven placemats and colored napkins to match the wrapped jug.

Vegetable Bread

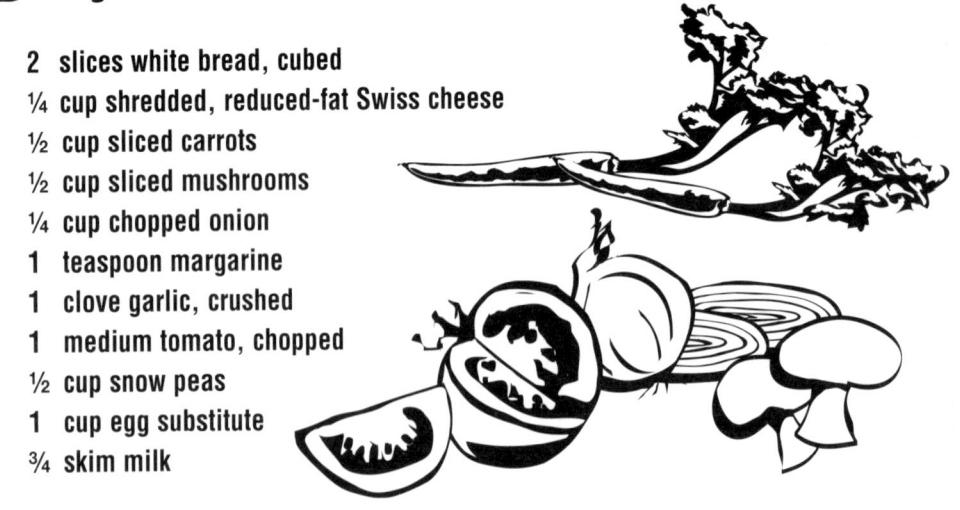

- 2 slices white bread, cubed
- ¼ cup shredded, reduced-fat Swiss cheese
- ½ cup sliced carrots
- ½ cup sliced mushrooms
- ¼ cup chopped onion
- 1 teaspoon margarine
- 1 clove garlic, crushed
- 1 medium tomato, chopped
- ½ cup snow peas
- 1 cup egg substitute
- ¾ skim milk

Preheat oven to 375°F.

Place bread cubes evenly on bottom of greased, 2-quart casserole dish. Sprinkle with cheese; set aside.

In medium nonstick skillet over medium heat, saute carrots, mushrooms, onion, and garlic in margarine until tender. Stir in tomato and snow peas; cook 1 to 2 minutes more. Spoon over cheese.

In a small bowl, combine egg substitute and milk; pour over vegetable mixture. Bake for 45–50 minutes or until knife inserted in center comes out clean. Let stand 10 minutes before serving. Serves 6.

Nutritional Information

Information per serving (6 servings)

Calories	104	Percentage of Calories from Carbohydrates: 31%
Carbohydrates	8 gm	Percentage of Calories from Protein: 35%
Protein	9 gm	Percentage of Calories from Fat: 34%
Fat	4 gm	
Cholesterol	6 mg	DIABETIC EXCHANGES
Sodium	219 mg	Carbohydrate: 0.5
Fiber	1 gm	Protein: 1
Calcium	126 mg	Fat: 1
Iron	1 mg	
Vitamin A	4147 IU	
Vitamin C	8 mg	

Real Style

Buy a round loaf of hard-crusted bread from the bakery department. Prepare for centerpiece by cutting a circle in the top of the loaf, lifting it out of the center. Place a clear container in the cut-out circle. Fill the container with fresh flowers and vegetables. The vegetables can be held in place by placing them on cut wooden skewers. Use linen or paper colorful napkins with everyday dishes.

Spinach Lasagna

Courtesy of Melissa Donaldson, R.D., Heart College @ HealthSouth Medical Center

1	package frozen spinach, thawed
¼	cup egg substitute
1	cup water
16	ounces 1% cottage cheese
3	cups shredded skim milk mozzarella (reserve ½ cup for topping)
4	cups no-salt-added tomato sauce (add dash of garlic powder)
16	ounces lasagna noodles, uncooked
1	tablespoon parsley flakes
1	teaspoon oregano
1	teaspoon basil
½	teaspoon salt
1	teaspoon pepper

Preheat oven to 350°F.

In a large bowl, mix together spinach, egg substitute, water, cheeses.

Spread a thin layer of tomato sauce in bottom of 9x13-inch baking pan. Place a layer of uncooked noodles over sauce. Pour 1½ cups of sauce over noodles.

Spread with half of the spinach mixture. Layer noodles over mixture and repeat layers. Finish with sauce on top layer.

Cover tightly with foil. Bake for 1 hour 15 minutes. Remove from oven and sprinkle with reserved mozzarella cheese. Return to oven for 5 minutes.

Remove from oven and allow to stand 15–20 minutes. Makes 12 servings.

Nutritional Information

Information per serving (12 servings)

Calories	262	Percentage of Calories from Carbohydrates: 49%
Carbohydrates	32 gm	Percentage of Calories from Protein: 30%
Protein	20 gm	Percentage of Calories from Fat: 21%
Fat	6 gm	
Cholesterol	19 mg	DIABETIC EXCHANGES
Sodium	484 mg	Carbohydrates: 2
Fiber	3 gm	Protein: 3
Calcium	314 mg	Fat: 1
Iron	3 mg	
Vitamin A	3044 IU	
Vitamin C	15 mg	

Zesty Grilled Chicken

- 4 chicken legs
- 4 chicken thighs
- 4 chicken wings
- 4 chicken breasts
- 1 16-ounce jar Italian fat-free dressing
- 1 cup barbeque sauce
- ½ cup Moore's Marinade™
- ¼ cup hot sauce

Rinse chicken and pat dry. Slice into thickest portions of the legs, thighs, and breasts 2–3 times. This aids in the cooking process and exposes more chicken to the sauce.

Mix remaining ingredients in a 4-quart mixing bowl. Reserve 1 cup in a separate bowl.

Add one piece of chicken at a time to the sauce, carefully mixing to coat each piece. When all of the chicken is mixed into the sauce, cover and allow chicken to marinate in the refrigerator for 2 hours.

Grill chicken on low to medium heat. The key to grilled chicken is cooking it slowly and turning it often. Use the reservd marinade to baste the chicken as you turn when it appears to be getting dry. Serves 8.

Nutritional Information

Information per serving (8 servings)

Calories	345
Carbohydrates	13 gm
Protein	53 gm
Fat	9 gm
Cholesterol	161 mg
Sodium	1323 mg
Fiber	1 gm
Calcium	35 mg
Iron	3 mg
Vitamin A	551 IU
Vitamin C	8 mg

Percentage of Calories from Carbohydrates: 15%
Percentage of Calories from Protein: 61%
Percentage of Calories from Fat: 24%

DIABETIC EXCHANGES
Carbohydrate: 1
Protein: 7.5
Fat: 2

Beef and Rice

- 1 pound ground beef
- 2 tablespoons butter
- 1 medium onion, diced
- 1 medium green pepper, chopped
- ½ cup converted rice
- 1 teaspoon salt
- ¼ teaspoon pepper
- 1 6-ounce can tomato paste
- 2 cups hot water

Preheat oven to 350°F.

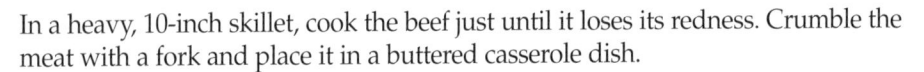

In a heavy, 10-inch skillet, cook the beef just until it loses its redness. Crumble the meat with a fork and place it in a buttered casserole dish.

In a separate skillet, melt 1 tablespoon of butter and cook the onion and green pepper until wilted. Add the vegetables to the beef.

In the same skillet, cook the rice in the remaining butter, stirring constantly until golden. Add the rice to the beef, stir, and season with salt and pepper.

Blend together the tomato paste and water. Pour over the beef mixture. Do not stir. Bake about 1 hour until the rice is tender. Tomato mixture will be on top. Serves 6.

Nutritional Information

Information per serving (6 servings)

Calories	281	Percentage of Calories from Carbohydrates: 23%
Carbohydrates	16 gm	Percentage of Calories from Protein: 23%
Protein	16 gm	Percentage of Calories from Fat: 54%
Fat	17 gm	
Cholesterol	52 mg	DIABETIC EXCHANGES
Sodium	593 mg	Carbohydrate: 1
Fiber	1 gm	Protein: 2
Calcium	22 mg	Fat: 3
Iron	2 mg	
Vitamin A	482 IU	
Vitamin C	28 mg	

Real Style

Whip up a touch of the South for your next get together. This casserole is brimming with Southern hospitality. Toss a salad of prepackaged greens to pair with this beef and rice dish for a great tailgating party. Sports are almost a religion in the South so create a theme for a fun sports centerpiece. Place uncooked rice in a fruit jar or clear cylinder. A 6-inch container will take about ¾ pound of long grain white rice. Pour a very small amount of water into the rice, allowing room for expansion. Use small shakers and pennants collected from former events to stick into the rice. Pick greenery or purchase festive florals from your grocery floral department to add in rice. Place a miniature or toy basketball, football, or several golf balls at the base of the container. Purchase paper goods to match your team's colors.

Etiquette and style have always been a part of our family's lifestyle. As children our parents took advantage of their captive audience at the dinner table to teach us the proper way of dining. Our grandmothers taught us to sip our tea from china cups and about the importance of dressing for dinner. During my teenage years I accompanied my Grandmother Alice to visit my cousin—the king of rock and roll, Elvis Presley—at Graceland, where dinner was a formal affair. The lessons of childhood have served me well. We learned through real manners how to charm our guests, family, and friends. When we come together over a meal it is a special time, and we honor each other with the presentation of the food, the table, and ourselves.

Darlene and I first worked together in the 1980s on the syndicated television show, "Total Wellness for Women," which I co-hosted with internationally renowned psychologist, Dr. Judy Kuriansky. We needed a segment to introduce real style to our audiences and Darlene's name was recommended. There was an instant connection between us of admiration and respect, and we learned that we shared similar backgrounds in etiquette and style. Over the years we have created many seminars, for both women and men, on style and attitude.

We hope that you enjoy our recipes with etiquette and style.

—Edie Hand

Etiquette and Style

Place Settings

Real style begins with a properly set table . . .

Informal Place Setting

Water Goblet/ All-purpose Glass

Dinner Fork

Napkin

Soup Spoon

Salad Fork

Dinner Knife

Dinner Plate

Formal Place Setting

Napkins

The Bow

1. Fold napkin in quarters.
2. Fold sides to center. 
3. Pleat in quarters. 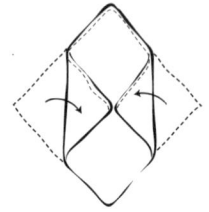 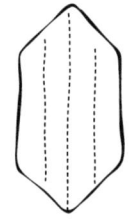
4. Tie with ribbon or slip on a ring.

Easy Elegance

1. Fold napkin in half.
2. Pleat into 1-inch accordion pleats.
3. Slip into wine glass and spread fan.

The Pocket

1. Fold napkin in half.
2. Fold top flap back one half.
3. Turn over and fold into quarters. 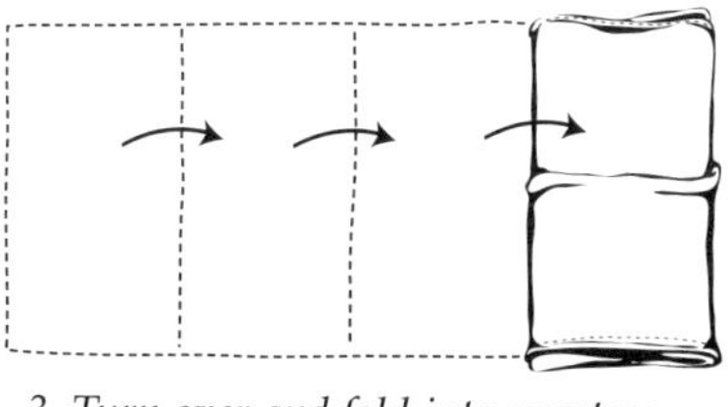
4. Insert utensils.

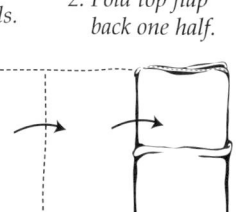

Quick and Easy

1. Fold napkin into quarters. 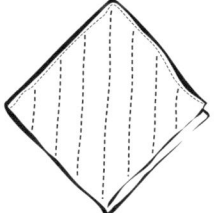
2. Fold in half.
3. Pleat each half.
4. Slip on a napkin ring.

The Basics of Dining Etiquette

Smart and Easy Etiquette Dining Tips

- Before salting or seasoning, taste your food to let the cook or chef know you believe in their cooking abilities. After tasting feel free to make slight adjustments.

- Buttering a whole roll or slice of bread is considered bad manners. Tear bread into bite-size pieces and butter one piece at a time.

- When coffee and tea are offered, its better to say "no thank you" than to turn your cup over in the saucer.

- When served soup, eat slowly and quietly from the side of your spoon. Fill your spoon by dipping the spoon forward away from you.

Smart and Easy Napkin Rules

- Napkin should be placed in your lap as soon as you are seated, in a restaurant, home, or boardroom.

- When temporarily leaving the table during a meal, place napkin to the right of your plate or on the arm or seat of your chair. Push your chair under the table upon walking away. Leave the table only if necessary.

- When completing the meal, follow your host's lead in placing your napkin to the left of your plate.

- When unfolding a large dinner napkin leave only one fold. Upon placing the napkin in your lap, the fold should face your waist.

- For a breakfast, luncheon, or brunch, small napkins can be completely unfolded and placed in your lap.

- Whether you received your folded napkin in your glass, on your plate, or to the left of your silver wear pick it up from the center. When you have finished eating, place it to the left of place setting. Do not refold.

The Etiquette of Passing Foods

- Family-style dining is passed from the left to the right. When being served by a server, food is presented on the left and removed on the right.

- When food is passed, allow the dish to be placed on the table before receiving.

- When passing the salt and pepper, they should be passed at the same time, not in the same hand, and placed on the table.

Limited Diet and Diabetic Guidelines

- Upon accepting an invitation, make your host or hostess aware of your dietary needs.

- When receiving an invitation to a restaurant, call and ask for special food accommodations, or if arrangements can be made upon your arrival.

- If you need to eat at certain intervals, be prepared for the cocktail hour and extended conversation before the meal is served.

Etiquette Tips for the Host, Hostess, and Guest

- Each guest is honoring the host and hostess by their presence. It is important to the guest to be acknowledged by the host or hostess, so greet guests warmly and verbalize how glad you are they came.

- Ask about special dietary needs for each guest.

- Plan and organize the menu in advance so you can be free to socialize.

- Make the stress of attending a special event easy on guests by seating people of like interests together.

- When planning the event menu, take into consideration the level of difficulty of the foods you choose.

Know Your Ingredients

Conversion Tables

Liquid Measures

American (Standard Cup) — Metric Equivalent

American (Standard Cup)	Metric Equivalent
1 teaspoon = 1/6 fluid ounce	5 ml
1 tablespoon = 1/2 fluid ounce	15 ml
1 cup = 1/2 pint = 8 fluid ounces	237 ml
1 pint = 16 fluid ounces	473 ml
1 quart = 2 pints = 32 fluid ounces	946 ml

British (Standard Cup) — Metric Equivalent

British (Standard Cup)	Metric Equivalent
1 teaspoon = 1/3 fluid ounce	6 ml
1 tablespoon = 0.55 fluid ounces	17 ml
1 cup = 1/2 pint = 10 fluid ounces	284 ml
1 pint = 20 fluid ounces	570 ml
1 quart = 2 pints = 40 fluid ounces	1.1 liter

1 cup = 16 tablespoons   1 tablespoon = 3 teaspoons

Solid Measures

American/British	Metric Equivalent
1 ounce	28 grams
3½ ounces	100 grams
1 pound = 16 ounces	453 grams
2.2 pounds	1000 grams = 1 kilogram

Oven Temperatures

Degrees Centigrade	Degrees Fahrenheit
Up to 105	Up to 225, cool
105–135	225–275, very slow
135–160	275–325, slow
175–190	350–375, moderate
215–230	400–450, hot
230–260	450–500, very hot
260	500, extremely hot

Recipe Modifications for Lowering Fat, Sugar, Salt, and Adding Fiber

Instead of:	Use:
1 whole egg	¼ cup egg substitute or 2 egg whites or 1 egg white plus 1 tsp oil
1 egg yolk	1 egg white
1 cup vegetable oil (can reduce by ⅓ in recipes)	1 cup olive or canola oil
1 cup butter (can reduce by ⅓ in recipes)	⅞ cup olive or canola oil or 1 cup liquid margarine or liquid Butter Buds
1 cup shortening (can reduce by ⅓ in recipes)	¾ cup olive or canola oil
½ cup shortening any oil in a baked recipe	⅓ cup olive or canola oil or same amount of moist food such as applesauce, yogurt, or prunes
1 cup whole milk	1 cup skim or nonfat buttermilk
1 cup buttermilk	1 tablespoon lemon juice or vinegar and skim milk to make 1 cup

Instead of:	Use:
1 cup light cream	1 cup fat-free half & half or 1 cup evaporated skim milk
1 cup sour cream or 1 cup cream cheese	1 cup fat-free sour cream or 1 cup plain, low-fat yogurt
1 cup thin white sauce	1 tablespoon oil plus 1 tablespoon flour plus 1 cup skim milk
1 cup medium white sauce	2 tablespoons oil plus 4 tablespoons flour plus 1 cup skim milk
1 cup thick white sauce	3 tablespoons oil plus 4 tablespoons flour plus 1 cup skim milk
cream soups	1 cup thin white sauce plus ¼ cup celery, 1 cup mushrooms and ⅕ chicken bouillon cube or reduced fat canned soups
1 cup white flour	1 cup minus 2 tablespoons whole wheat flour, and decrease oil in recipe by 1 tablespoon and increase liquid by 1–2 teaspoons, or use ½ cup white plus ½ cup wheat
mayonnaise	yogurt or fat free/low fat mayonnaise
sugar	Can generally be reduced by ½ in recipes

Carbohydrate Exchanges

Bread

One bread exchange equals:
15 grams carbohydrates, 3 grams protein, 0–1 gram fat and 80 calories

bagel	½ (1 ounce)
Bread, reduced-calorie	2 slices (1½ ounces)
Bread, white, whole-wheat, pumpernickel, rye	1 slice (1 ounce)
Bread sticks, crisp, 4 in. long x ½ in.	2 (⅔ ounce)
English muffin	½
Hot dog or hamburger bun	½ (1 ounce)
Pita, 6 in. across	½
Roll, plain, small	1 (1 ounce)
Raisin Bread, unfrosted	1 slice (1 ounce)
Tortilla, 6 in. across, corn or flour	1
Waffle, 4½ in. square, reduced-fat	1

Starchy Vegetables

One starchy vegetable exchange equals:
15 grams carbohydrates, 3 grams protein, 0–1 gram fat and 80 calories

Baked beans	⅓ cup
Corn	½ cup
Corn on cob, medium	1 (5 ounces)
Mixed vegetables with corn, peas, or pasta	1 cup
Peas, green	½ cup
Plantain	½ cup
Potato, baked or boiled	1 small (3 ounces)
Potato mashed	½ cup
Squash, winter (acorn, butternut, pumpkin)	1 cup
Yam (sweet potato), plain	½ cup

Nutrition Tips

1. Most starch choices are good sources of B vitamins.
2. Foods made from whole grains are good sources of fiber.
3. Beans, peas, and lentils are good source of protein and fiber.

Fruit

One fruit exchange equals:
15 grams carbohydrates and 60 calories. The weight includes skin, core seeds, and rind.

Apple, unpeeled small	1 (4 ounces)
Applesauce, unsweetened	½ cup
Apples dried	4 rings
Apricots, fresh	4 whole (5½ ounces)
Apricots, dried	8 halves
Apricots, canned	½ cup
Banana, small	1 (4 ounces)
Blackberries	¾ cup
Blueberries	¾ cup
Cantaloupe, small	⅓ melon (11 ounces) or 1 cup cubes
Cherries, sweet fresh	12 (3 ounces)
Cherries, sweet canned	½ cup
Dates	3

Figs, fresh	1½ large or 2 medium (3½ ounces)
Figs, dried	½ cup
Fruit Cocktail	½ cup
Grapefruit, large	½ (11 ounces)
Grapefruit sections, canned	¾ cup
Grapes, small	17 (3 ounces)
Honeydew melon	1 slice (10 ounces) or 1 cup cubes
Kiwi	1 (3½ ounces)
Mandarin oranges, canned	¾ cup
Mango, small	½ fruit (5½ ounces) or ½ cup
Nectarine, small	1 (5 ounces)
Orange, small	1 (6½ ounces)
Papaya	½ fruit (8 ounces) or 1 cup cubes
Peaches, canned	½ cup
Pear, large fresh	½ (4 ounces)
Pear, canned	½ cup

Pineapple, fresh	¾ cup
Pineapple, canned	½ cup
Plums, small	2 (5 ounces)
Plums, canned	½ cup
Prunes, dried	3
Raisins	2 tablespoons
Raspberries	1 cup
Strawberries	1¼ cup whole berries
Tangerines, small	2 (8 ounces)
Watermelon	1 slice (13½ ounces) or 1¼ cup cubes

Fruit Juices

Apple juice/cider	½ cup
Cranberry juice cocktail	⅓ cup
Cranberry juice cocktail, reduced-calorie	1 cup
Fruit juice blends, 100% juice	⅓ cup

Grape juice	⅓ cup
Grapefruit juice	½ cup
Orange juice	½ cup
Pineapple juice	½ cup
Prune juice	⅓ cup

Nutrition Tips

1. Fresh, frozen, and dried fruits have about 2 grams of fiber per choice. Fruit juices contain very little fiber.

2. Citrus fruits, berries, and melons are good sources of Vitamin C.

Milk

Milk and milk products are on this list. You'll find cheeses on the Meat List and cream and other dairy fats on the Fat List. Based on the amount of fat they contain, milks are divided into fat-free/low-fat, reduced-fat, and whole milk. One choice includes the following nutritional information.

	Carbohydrate (grams)	Protein (grams)	Fat (grams)	Calories
Fat-free/low-fat	12	8	0–3	90
Reduced-fat	12	8	5	120
Whole	12	8	8	150

One Milk Exchange equals: 12 grams carbohydrate and 8 grams protein

Fat-free and Low-Fat Milk (0–3 grams fat per serving)

Fat-free, ½%, or 1% milk	1 cup
Fat-free or low fat buttermilk	1 cup
Evaporated fat-free milk	½ cup
Fat-free dry milk	⅓ cup dry
Plain nonfat yogurt	¾ cup
Nonfat or low-fat fruit-flavored yogurt sweetened with aspartame or with a non-nutritive sweetener	1 cup

Reduced-Fat Milk (5 grams fat per serving)

2% milk	1 cup
Plain low-fat yogurt	¾ cup
Sweeter acidophilus milk	1 cup

Whole Milk (8 grams fat per serving)

Whole milk	1 cup
Evaporated whole milk	½ cup
Goat's milk	1 cup
Kefir	1 cup

Nutrition Tips

1. Milk and yogurt are good sources of calcium and protein.

2. The higher the fat content of milk and yogurt, the greater the amount of saturated fat and cholesterol. Choose lower-fat varieties.

3. For those who are lactose intolerant, look for lactose-reduced or lactose-free varieties of milk.

Fats

One fat exchange equals: 5 grams fat and 45 calories

Monounsaturated Fats List

Avocado, medium	⅛ (1 ounce)
Nuts	
almonds, cashews	6 nuts
mixed (50% peanuts)	6 nuts
peanuts	10 nuts
pecans	4 halves
Oil (canola, olive, peanut)	1 teaspoon
Olives — ripe (black) green, stuffed*	10 large
Peanut butter, smooth or crunchy	2 teaspoons
Sesame seeds	1 tablespoon
Tahini paste	2 teaspoons

Polyunsaturated Fats

Margarine — stick, tub, or squeeze	1 tablespoon
Lower-fat (30% to 50% vegetable oil)	1 tablespoon
Mayonnaise — regular	1 teaspoon
reduced-fat	1 tablespoon
Nuts — walnuts English	4 halves
oil (corn, safflower, soybean)	1 teaspoon
Salad dressing — regular*	1 tablespoon
reduced-fat	2 tablespoons
Miracle Whip Salad Dressing — regular	2 teaspoons
reduced-fat	1 tablespoon
Seeds — pumpkin, sunflower	1 tablespoon

* 400 mg or more sodium per exchange.

Saturated Fats

Bacon, cooked	1 slice (20 slices/pound)
Bacon, grease	1 teaspoon
Butter, stick	1 teaspoon
whipped	2 teaspoons
reduced-fat	1 tablespoon
Chitterlings, boiled	2 tablespoons (½ ounce)
Coconut sweetened, shredded	2 tablespoons
Cream half and half	2 tablespoons
Cream cheese: regular	1 tablespoon (½ ounce)
reduced-fat	2 tablespoons (1 ounce)
Shortening or lard	1 teaspoon
Sour cream — regular	2 tablespoons
reduced-fat	3 tablespoons

Nutrition Tips

1. All fats are high in calories. Limit serving sizes for good nutrition and health.

2. Nuts and seeds contain a small amount of fiber, protein, and magnesium.

3. If blood pressure is a concern, choose fats in the unsalted form to help lower sodium intake, such as unsalted peanuts.

4. When selecting regular margarine, choose those with liquid vegetable oil as the first ingredient. Soft margarines are not as saturated as stick margarines. Avoid those listing hydrogenated or partially hydrogenated fat as the first ingredient.

5. When cooking with fatback or salt pork, use a piece 1 in. x 1in. x ¼ in. if you plan to eat the fatback cooked with vegetables. Use a piece 2 in. x 1 in. x ½ in. when eating only the vegetables with the fatback removed. Saturated fat can raise blood cholesterol levels.

Nutrition Tips 1–4 courtesy workshop booklet, Heart College at HealthSouth.

Very Lean Meat, Fish, and Substitutes

One protein exchange equals:
7 grams of protein, 0–1 gram of fat, and 0 carbohydrate

Poultry — chicken or turkey (white meat, no skin) Cornish hen (no skin)	1 ounce
Fish — fresh or frozen cod, flounder, haddock, halibut, trout, tuna fresh or canned in water	1 ounce
Shellfish — clams, crab, lobster, scallops, shrimp, imitation shellfish	1 ounce
Game — duck or pheasant (no skin), venison, buffalo, ostrich	1 ounce
Cheese with 1 gram or less fat per ounce, nonfat or low-fat cottage cheese	¼ cup
Fat-free cheese	1 ounce
Other — processed sandwich meats with 1 gram or less fat per ounce, such as deli thin shaved meats, chipped beef*, turkey, ham	1 ounce
Egg whites	2

Egg substitutes, plain	¼ cup
Hot dogs with 1 gram or less fat per ounce*	1 ounce
Kidney (high in cholesterol)	1 ounce
Sausage with 1 gram or less fat per ounce	1 ounce

Nutrition Tips
1. Choose very lean and lean meats whenever possible. Items from the high-fat group are high in saturated fat, cholesterol, and calories, and can raise blood cholesterol levels.

2. Meats do not have any fiber.

3. Some processed meats, seafood, and soy products may contain carbohydrates when consumed in large amounts. Check the nutrition facts on the label to see if the amount is close to 15 grams. If so, count it as carbohydrate choice as well as a meat choice.

---

* 400 mg or more sodium per exchange.

Lean Meat

One protein exchange equals:
7 grams protein, 3 grams fat, 0 grams carbohydrate, and 55 calories

Beef — USDA select or choice grades of lean beef trimmed of fat, such as round, sirloin, and flank steak; tenderloin; roast (rib chuck rump) steak (T-bone, porterhouse, cubed); grounded round	1 ounce
Pork — lean pork, such as fresh ham, canned, cured, or boiled ham; Canadian bacon*; tenderloin center loin chop	1 ounce
Lamb — roast, chop, leg	1 ounce
Veal — lean chop, leg	1 ounce
Poultry — chicken, turkey (dark meat no skin), chicken (white meat with skin), domestic duck or goose (well-drained of fat, no skin)	1 ounce
Fish — Herring (uncreamed or smoked)	1 ounce
Oysters	6 medium
Salmon (fresh or canned), catfish	1 ounce

Sardines (canned)	2 medium
Tuna (canned in oil drained)	1 ounce
Game — Goose (no skin), rabbit	1 ounce
Cheese — 4.5%-fat cottage cheese	¼ cup
Grated Parmesan	2 tablespoons
Cheeses with 3 grams or less fat per ounce	1 ounce
Hot dogs* with 3 grams or less fat per ounce	1½ ounces
Processed sandwich meat with 3 grams or less fat per ounce, such as turkey, pastrami, or kielbasa	1 ounce
Liver, heart (high in cholesterol)	1 ounce

Count as one very lean meat and one starch exchange

Bean, peas*, lentils (cooked)	½ cup

*400 mg or more sodium per exchange.

Healthy Cooking Tips

1. Experiment with recipes. At first, use about ¾ of the fat suggested in the recipe. Next time reduce the amount of fat to half. Many recipes include more fat than is necessary. Although extra virgin olive oil has a strong taste, try it in recipes. Much of its flavor disappears when cooked, especially when cutting back on the amount of oil suggested. Light olive oils will provide the same monounsaturated fat and have a lighter flavor, if you find the extra virgin olive oil in a particular recipe objectionable.

2. Since you may lose some moisture when you reduce the amount of fat in some recipes, consider adding defatted chicken broth, skim milk, wine, fruit juice, yogurt, or applesauce when appropriate.

3. Use nonstick pots and pans for preparing pancakes, omelets, and sauteed vegetables, and coat the pan with a nonstick vegetable oil spray, to avoid using (as much) oil.

4. Steam or microwave vegetables or saute in broth. For flavor, toss with a few drops of olive oil, or a small amount of grated low-fat cheese.

About the Authors

Edie Hand

Edie Hand is a radio and television personality seen on the Food Network and regional and national television morning show cooking segments, and has toured for Unilever/Bestfoods on their "Good to Know Ya Tour" across the Southeast. She is co-host of the "News U Can Use" radio show with Ken Glickman, and is a member of American Women in Radio & Television, National Speakers Associations, and a co-founder of RealHand Approaches' " Styling with Attitude on a Budget" cooking seminars and special events. Edie is also the founder of the Edie Hand Foundation to benefit Alabama and national charities. The author and co-author of six books and mother to one son, Edie lives near Birmingham, Alabama, with her husband, Coach Mark Aldridge.

Darlene Real

Darlene Real is a professional speaker, author, and photography stylist, specializing in food, fashion, and furnishings. She is the founder of Appearance Matters, Inc. and co-developer RealHand Approaches' "Styling with Attitude on a Budget" cooking seminars and special events. Darlene coaches corporate and business clients to enhance their appearance through image and etiquette. She has three children and lives in Birmingham, Alabama.

Photo by billybrown.com

Debra Lustrea

Debra Lustrea is a first-generation American businesswoman who has experienced success in many areas. She is a strong advocate for families and children with disabilities and works with communities to create programs to help meet their special needs. Debra promotes alternative dispute resolution through the company she developed with a nationally renowned negotiator and also founded Women Developing Leadership, a group of women, executives, and entrepreneurs who work with women in crisis to redevelop mind, body, and soul. In addition, Debra has an executive position at a Chicago boutique financial brokerage clearing house. She resides near Chicago, Illinois, where she shares her love of cooking with her family.

Photo by Todd Rennels